SCROLL SAW
POLICE & RESCUE

Patterns

by Mike and Vicky Lewis

Fox
Chapel Publishing Co. Inc.

1970 Broad Street • East Petersburg, PA 17520 • www.carvingworld.com

© 2002 Fox Chapel Publishing Co., Inc.

Scroll Saw Police and Rescue Patterns is a brand new work, first published in 2002 by Fox Chapel Publishing Company, Inc. The patterns contained herein are copyrighted by the author. Artists purchasing this book have permission to make up to 200 cutouts of each individual pattern. Persons or companies wishing to make more than 200 cutouts must notify the author for permission. The patterns themselves, however, are not to be duplicated for resale or distribution under any circumstances.

Dog patterns used with permission from *Fine Line Designs Dog Breeds* © Judy Gale Roberts.
Rescue Three FDNY (on our front cover) scrolled by David Penman.

Publisher . . . . .Alan Giagnocavo
Editor . . . . .Ayleen Stellhorn
Desktop Specialist . . . . .Linda L. Eberly, Eberly Designs Inc.
Cover Design and Photography . . . . .Keren Holl

ISBN 1–56523–157–0
Library of Congress Card Number 2002102482

To order your copy of this book,
please remit the cover price
plus $3 shipping to:
Fox Chapel Publishing Company
Book Orders
1970 Broad Street
East Petersburg, PA 17520

Or visit us on the web at
www.foxchapelpublishing.com

Manufactured in the United States
10 9 8 7 6 5 4 3 2 1

TABLE OF CONTENTS

ABOUT THE AUTHORS
Mike and Vicky Lewis

Mike Lewis, an Army Veteran, has been perfecting his scroll saw techniques since 1987. What started as a hobby for Mike has now become a very rewarding career, progressing from basic scroll work projects to recreating his own designs and teaching.

Vicky began scrolling in 1998 to help Mike. This quickly became a passion for her. Cutting almost daily, she quickly realized their scroll saw could be used not only to cut elegant Victorian scroll work, but also to cut the many wood items and personal designs that are displayed in their shop.

Currently, both Mike and Vicky are demonstrating craftsmen and teachers at Dollywood Theme Park in Pigeon Forge, Tennessee. Their shop, Sawdust and Shavings, is located in the Craftsman's Valley inside the park. For more information about classes and scroll work, contact Mike and Vicky directly at (865) 428–9401 or e-mail them at *mlewis58@bellsouth.net*. Mail can be sent to their home at 1053 Valley View Circle, Seviersville, TN 37876.

HELPFUL HINTS

Listed below are suggested and helpful hints that can be used when cutting the designs in this book. Use whatever materials, sizes and techniques best suit your needs.

Materials

We suggest ⅛ inch to ¼ inch birch plywood or Baltic birch plywood, along with any hardwood. Select your wood with care. Wood should be "clean" on both sides. We do not suggest using pine to cut any of the designs shown in this book.

Design Layout

There are several methods that can be used to lay out the designs in this book. You can use the method suggested here or one that you find has worked well for you in the past.

First, always make a photocopy of the original design you are going to cut. This saves your master copy for future use. You can reduce or enlarge the designs as necessary on a photocopier or by scanning the pattern into a computer program that will allow you to scale the design.

Then, use a repositioning spray glue on the back side of the pattern to adhere the design to the face of the wood. You can determine the "face" of the wood by looking for the best grain lines and no flaws. Spray the paper—not the wood—and spray lightly.

Blades

We use #5, #2 and #2/0 reverse teeth blades. The reverse teeth blades help to keep the wood from fraying on the back side and clean up any inside cut areas. The #2/0R saw blades are used to cut all accent and detail lines in all of the designs, such as wings and other areas indicated by solid black lines.

Cutting Tips

Depending on the material thickness, stack two to four pieces of wood at a time. Secure the pieces with nail brads placed in each of the four corners of the wood and in scrap areas to be cut out. Secure one corner with three brads to form a triangle in that corner.

As a general rule, cut the most delicate areas first. This includes all the accent and detail lines in each design. Solid lines outside the cut areas indicating accent or detail lines should be cut also.

Cut out all of the waste areas. Leave cuts marked with an arrow until last, then cut away the center circle first followed by the inside rope area.

The last area to be cut should be the outside rope. Cutting in a counter-clockwise motion and starting at the triangle corner, begin cutting the outside rope areas around to the halfway point. Cut the scrap away and add in the detail lines that define the rope.

Begin cutting the second half of the outside rope, also in a counter-clockwise motion, up toward the corner with the three nails. Stop about an inch or two before the rope is completely cut out. Then cut the detail lines that define the rope.

At this point, you should have approximately three to seven scalloped edges left to cut. Begin cutting the remaining section in a clock-wise motion, making sure to cut the accent lines at the same time that you are making the scalloped cut. Continue cutting until the rope has been completely cut away from the corner.

Finishing Tips

Remove the pattern carefully from the wood. Use a pocket knife to gently lift a pattern that is difficult to remove. Sand and stain the finished piece to suit.

1

After the piece has dried, reassemble the three rings by turning the pieces face down. The second ring is elevated by small ⅛ inch pieces of wood called spacers. Use at least four spacers to elevate this ring. The outside rope is elevated by ¼ inch spacers. Use at least four spacers to elevate this ring also. The center ring lies flat on the work surface.

Glue along each ring edge. Let the glue dry completely before lifting the piece.

A wood back can be added to the back of any design to add color and dimension to your cut piece. Be sure the diameter of this back is cut small enough to fit inside the scallops of the rope-cut edge. Pieces can also be placed in shadow boxes.

Personalization

Each design can be personalized using the alphabet circle and the number circle located in the back of this book. Try adding a name or a division. You can also add dates of service and other personal information.

When you personalize a design, make sure the names and ranks, along with dates and other personal information, are centered to guarantee total balance in the design.

Three circular lines are shown on the patterns in this book.

Line A is an aid for placing the letters on the pattern and should not be cut.
Line B is the line that separates the inner part of the design from the outer circle. Cut on this line.
Line C is an aid for placing the drawings on the inner circle of the pattern. Cut only where the line does not cross the design.

The centers of each pattern can be left whole or replaced with the state seals in the last section of this book.

K-9 UNIT
(GERMAN SHEPHERD)

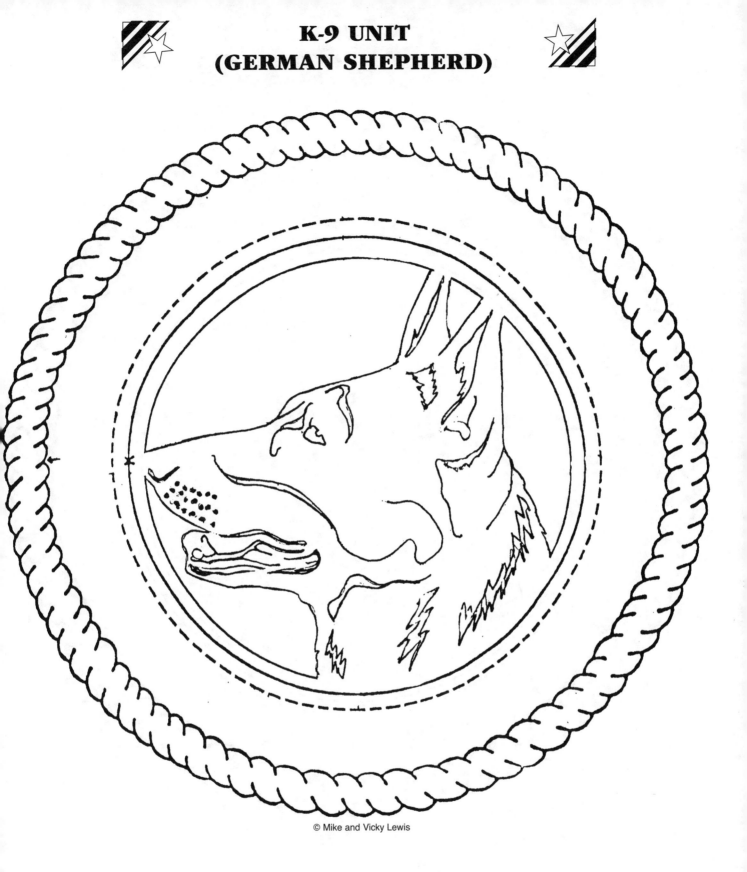

© Mike and Vicky Lewis

Scroll Saw Police and Rescue Patterns

© Mike and Vicky Lewis

© Mike and Vicky Lewis

Scroll Saw Police and Rescue Patterns

© Mike and Vicky Lewis

© Mike and Vicky Lewis

© Mike and Vicky Lewis

© Mike and Vicky Lewis

DECORATIVE FIVE POINT STAR

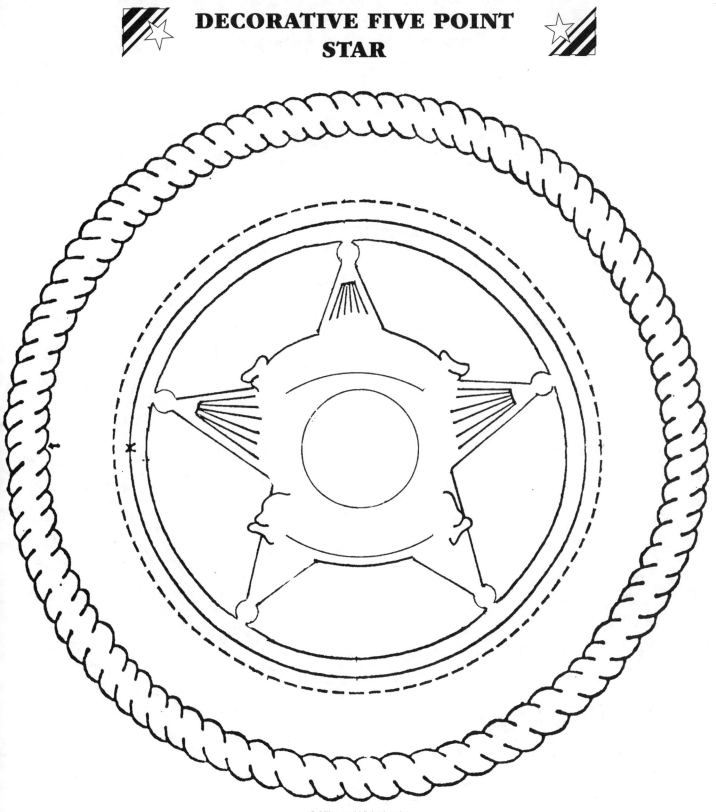

13

Scroll Saw Police and Rescue Patterns

© Mike and Vicky Lewis

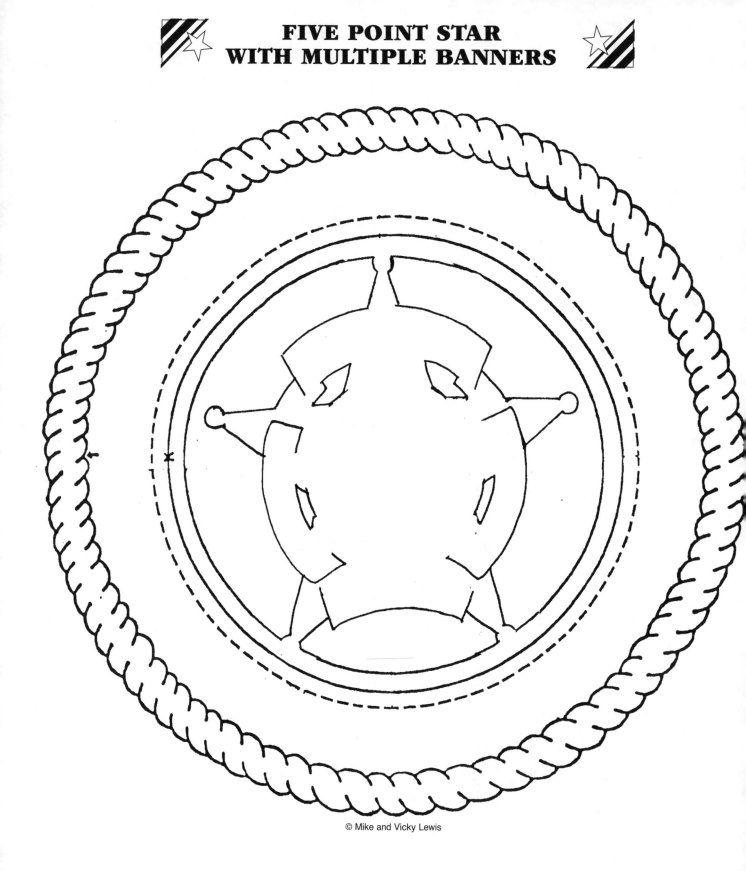

© Mike and Vicky Lewis

© Mike and Vicky Lewis

© Mike and Vicky Lewis

FIVE POINT STAR WITH
MAPLE LEAF ACCENTS

© Mike and Vicky Lewis

19

Scroll Saw Police and Rescue Patterns

© Mike and Vicky Lewis

© Mike and Vicky Lewis

© Mike and Vicky Lewis

FIVE POINT STAR
WITH EAGLE AND
MAPLE LEAF ACCENTS

© Mike and Vicky Lewis

FIVE POINT STAR
WITH ROPES

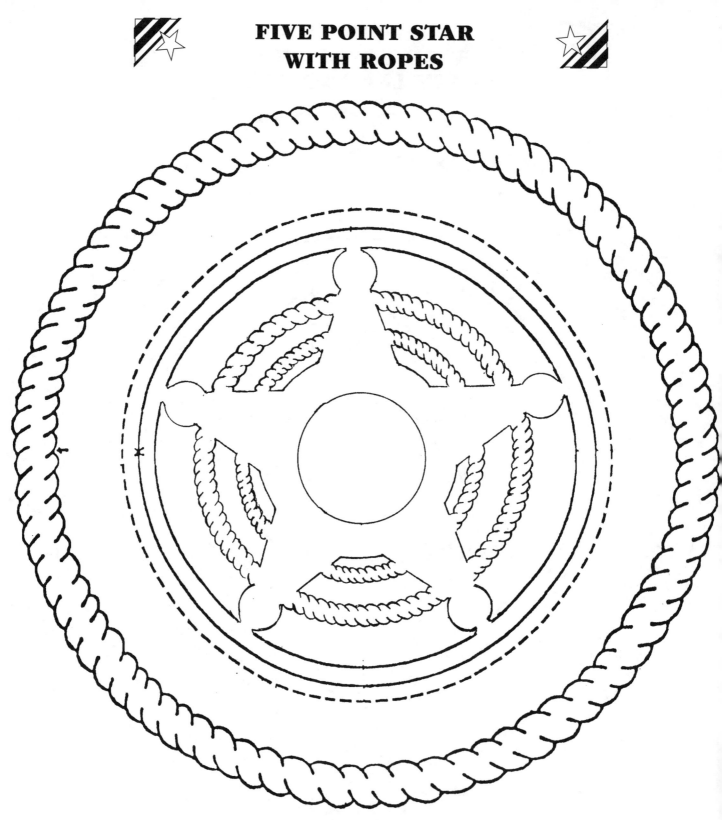

© Mike and Vicky Lewis

Scroll Saw Police and Rescue Patterns

© Mike and Vicky Lewis

SEVEN POINT STAR WITH TOBACCO LEAF POINTS

© Mike and Vicky Lewis

SEVEN POINT STAR WITH BANNER AND TOBACCO LEAF POINTS

© Mike and Vicky Lewis

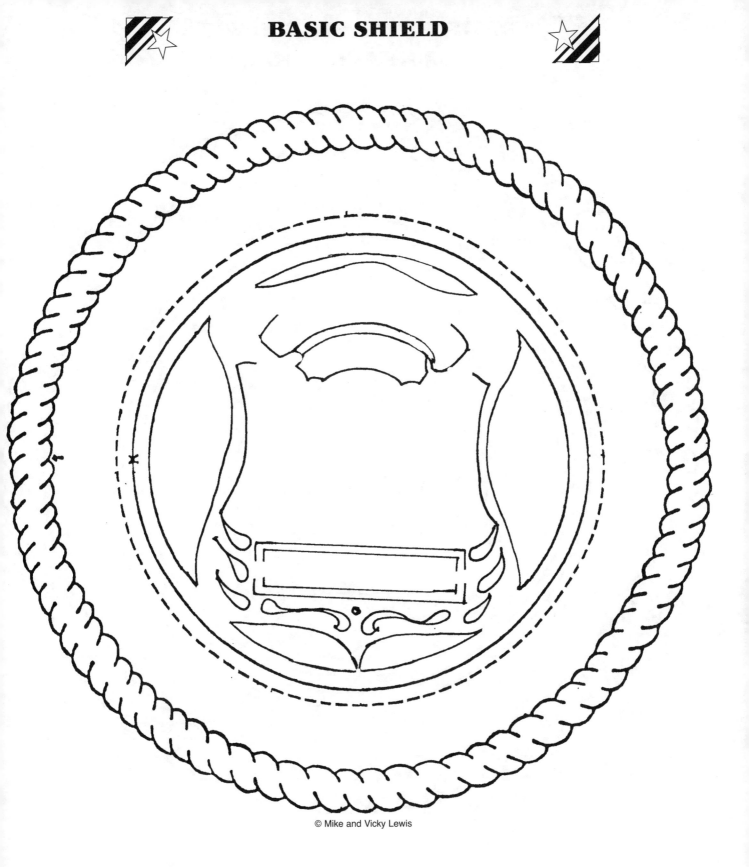

© Mike and Vicky Lewis

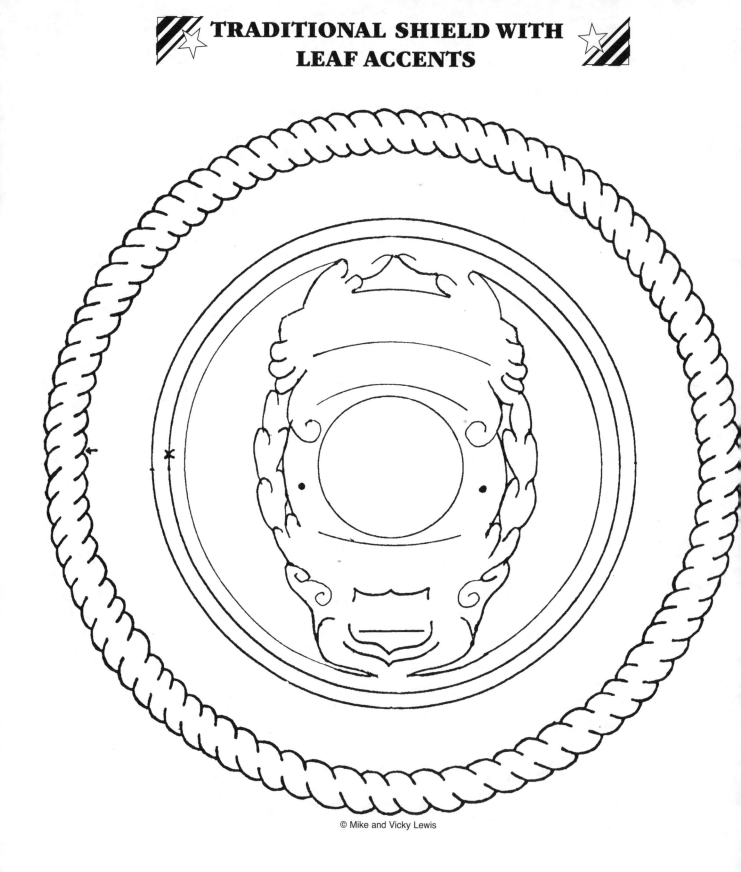

© Mike and Vicky Lewis

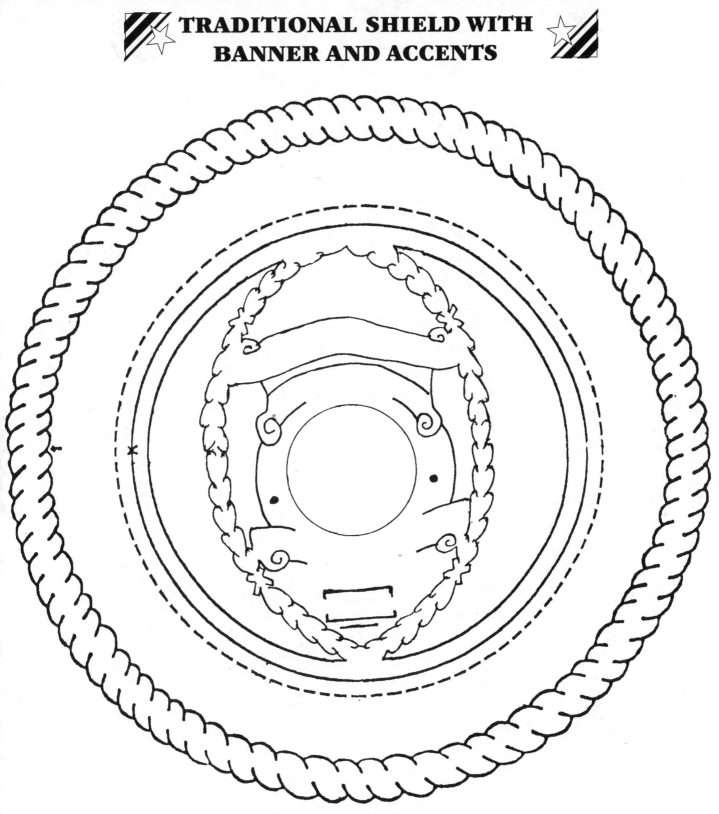

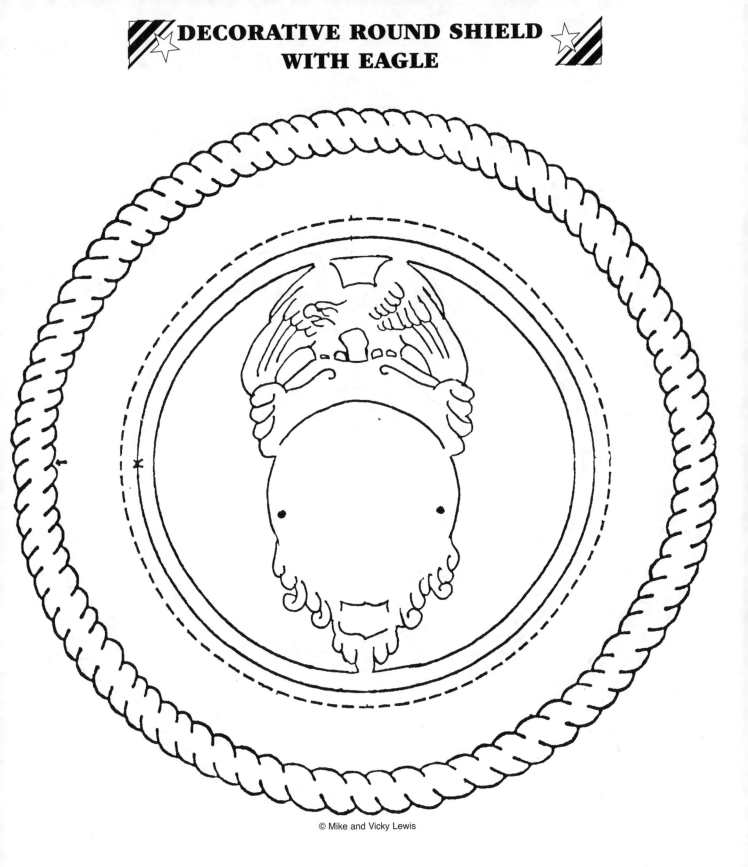

© Mike and Vicky Lewis

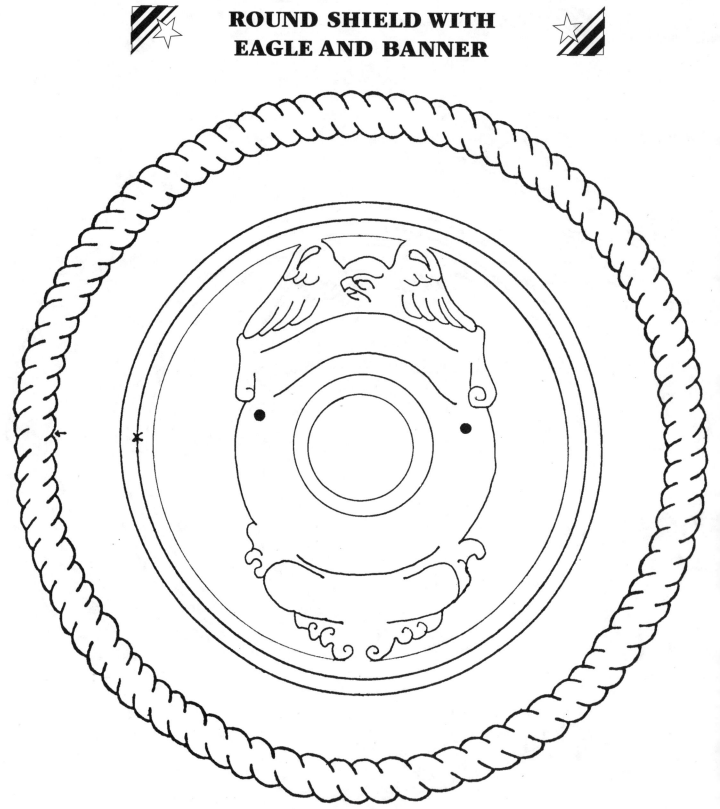

© Mike and Vicky Lewis

© Mike and Vicky Lewis

FANCY SHIELD
WITH EAGLE

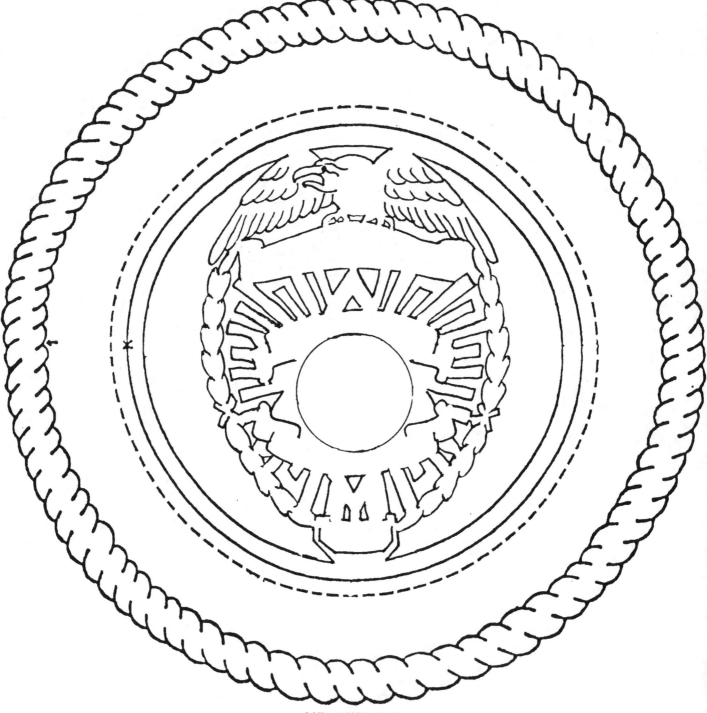

POINTED SHIELD
WITH EAGLE

Scroll Saw Police and Rescue Patterns

EAGLE SHIELD
WITH BURST

© Mike and Vicky Lewis

Scroll Saw Police and Rescue Patterns

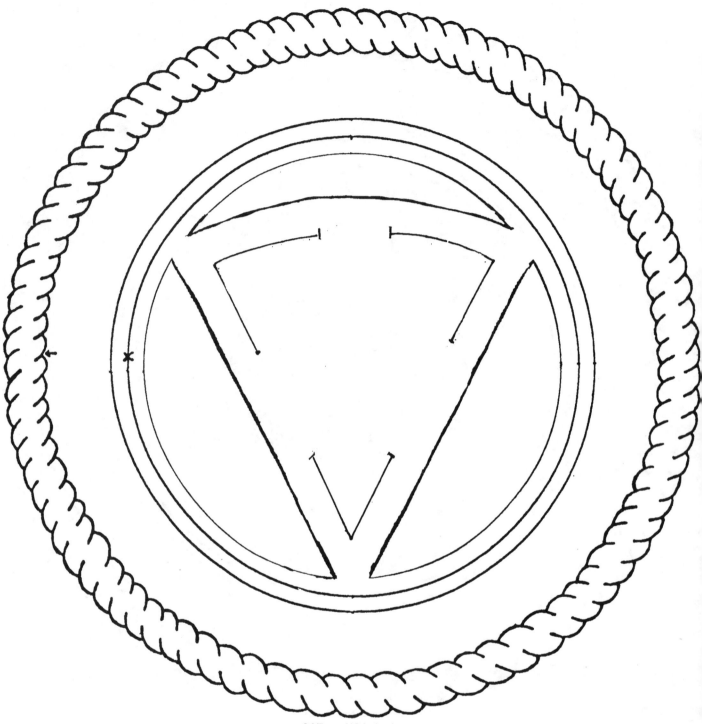

© Mike and Vicky Lewis

ALABAMA

ALASKA

ARIZONA

ARKANSAS

CALIFORNIA

COLORADO

STATE SEALS

CONNECTICUT

DELAWARE

D.C.

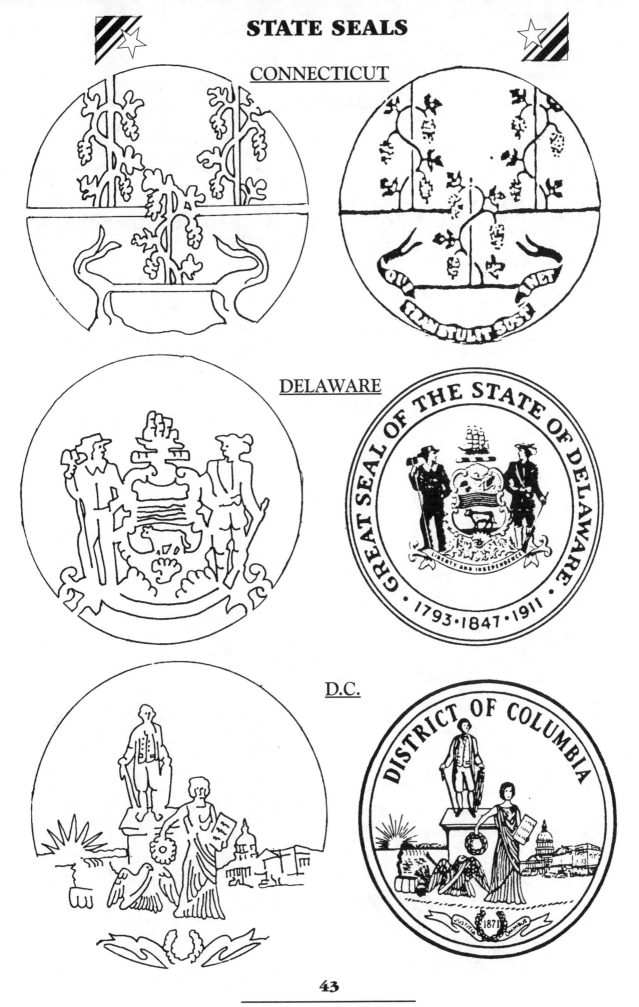

Scroll Saw Police and Rescue Patterns

FLORIDA

GEORGIA

HAWAII

IDAHO

ILLINOIS

INDIANA

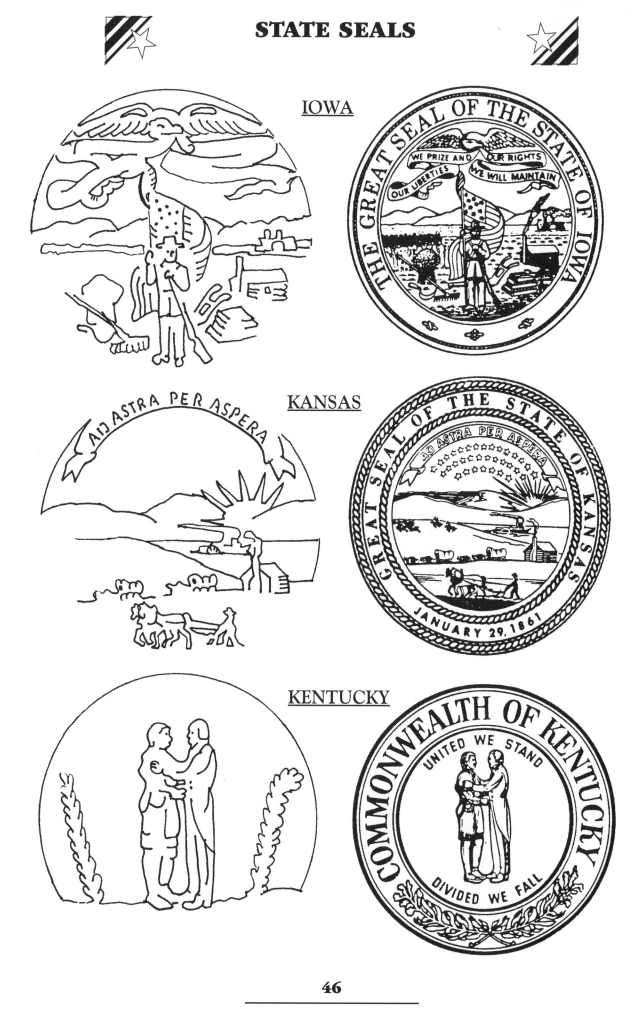

IOWA

KANSAS

KENTUCKY

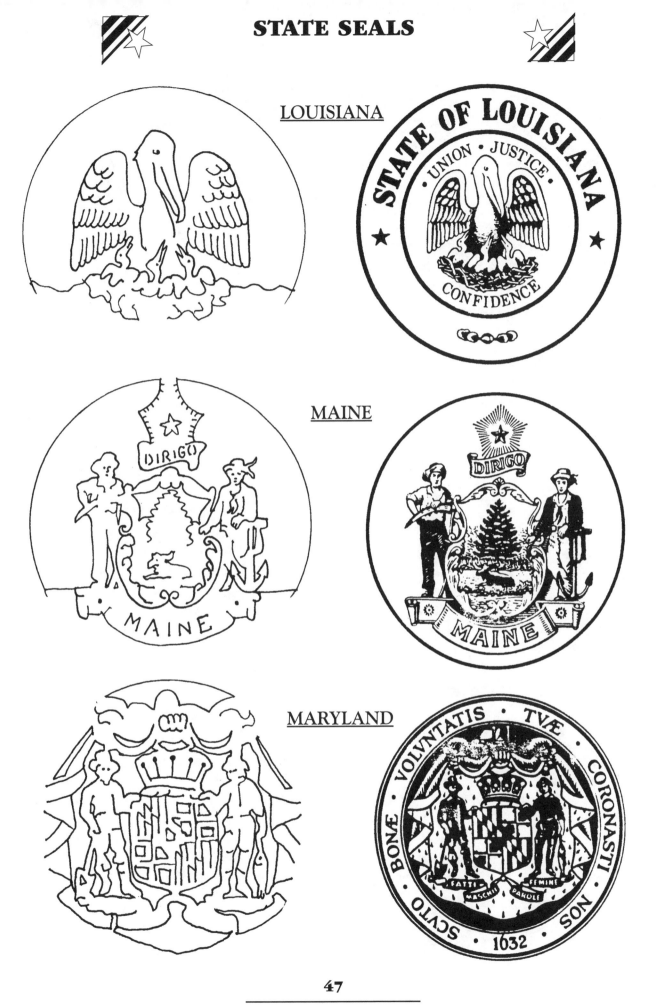

LOUISIANA

STATE OF LOUISIANA

UNION · JUSTICE

CONFIDENCE

MAINE

DIRIGO

MAINE

MARYLAND

VOLVNTATIS · TVÆ

SCVTO · BONE

CORONASTI · NOS

FATTI · MASCHII · PAROLE · FEMINE

1632

MISSISSIPPI

MONTANA

MISSOURI

MASSACHUSETTS

MICHIGAN

MINNESOTA

NEBRASKA

NEVADA

NEW
HAMPSHIRE

NORTH CAROLINA

NORTH DAKOTA

OHIO

NEW
JERSEY

NEW
MEXICO

NEW
YORK

OKLAHOMA

OREGON

PENNSYLVANIA

RHODE
ISLAND

SOUTH
CAROLINA

SOUTH
DAKOTA

54

TENNESSEE

TEXAS

UTAH

VERMONT

VIRGINIA

WASHINGTON

WISCONSIN

WEST
VIRGINIA

WYOMING

© Mike and Vicky Lewis

NUMBER WHEEL

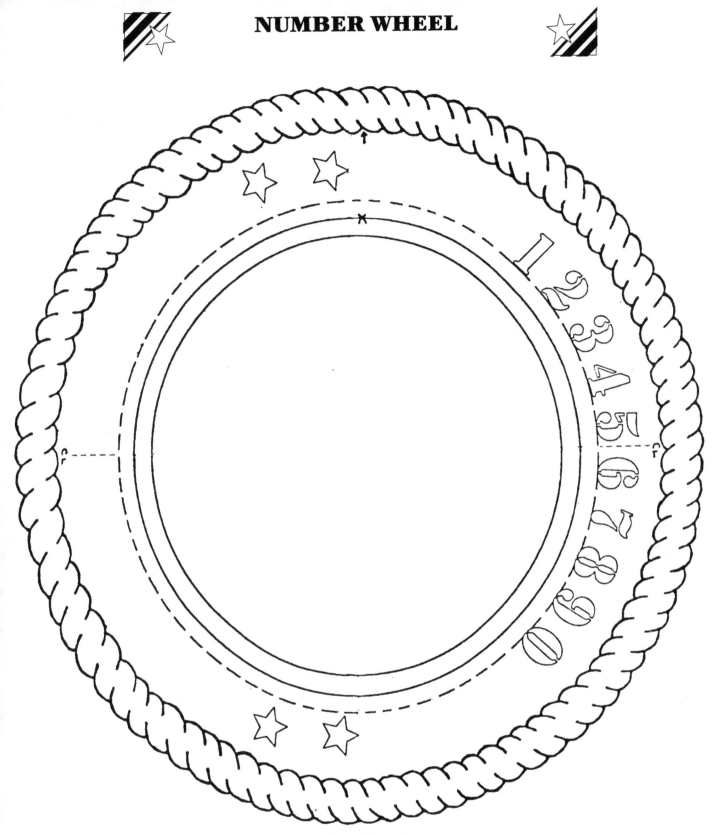

© Mike and Vicky Lewis

Scroll Saw Police and Rescue Patterns

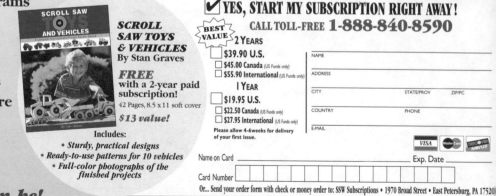

SUBSCRIBE TODAY!

DON'T MISS ANOTHER ISSUE OF SCROLL SAW WORKSHOP

☐ **ONE YEAR** Subscription

☐ $19.95 USA
☐ $22.50 Canada - US Funds Only
☐ $27.95 Int'l - US Funds Only

☐ **TWO YEAR** Subscription

☐ $39.90 USA
☐ $45.00 Canada - US Funds Only
☐ $55.90 Int'l - US Funds Only

Please allow 4-6 weeks for delivery

Four issues per year

☐ Bill Me   ☐ Check/Money Order
☐ Visa, MC or Discover

Name on card _____

Exp. date _____ Telephone ( ) _____
cardnumber

Send To:

Name: _____
Address: _____

City: _____
State/Prov.: _____
Zip: _____
Telephone: _____ Country: _____

VISA   MasterCard   DISCOVER NOVUS   CFBN

SCROLL SAW TOYS AND VEHICLES

FREE
with a two-year paid subscription

www.scrollsawer.com

Subscription order desk 888-840-8590

SUBSCRIBE TODAY!

DON'T MISS ANOTHER ISSUE OF WOOD CARVING ILLUSTRATED

☐ **ONE YEAR** Subscription

☐ $19.95 USA
☐ $22.50 Canada - US Funds Only
☐ $27.95 Int'l - US Funds Only

☐ **TWO YEAR** Subscription

☐ $39.90 USA
☐ $45.00 Canada - US Funds Only
☐ $55.90 Int'l - US Funds Only

Please allow 4-6 weeks for delivery

Four issues per year

☐ Bill Me   ☐ Check/Money Order
☐ Visa, MC or Discover

Name on card _____

Exp. date _____ Telephone ( ) _____
cardnumber

Send To:

Name: _____
Address: _____
_____
City: _____
State/Prov.: _____
Zip: _____
Telephone: _____ Country: _____

VISA   MasterCard   DISCOVER NOVUS   CFBN

Power Carving

FREE
with a two-year paid subscription

www.carvingworld.com

Subscription order desk: 888-506-6630

FREE BOOK CATALOG

YES! *I'd like a free catalog of your woodworking titles. Please place me on your mailing list and send me a copy right away.*

Previously purchased titles:
_____
_____

I'm particularly interested in: *(circle all that apply)*   General Woodworking   Woodcarving   Scroll Sawing   Cabinetmaking   Nature Drawing

Suggestion box: I think Fox Chapel should do a book about:
_____
_____

Bonus: Give us your email address to receive free updates.

Send to:
Name: _____   Email Address: _____
Address: _____   City: _____
State/Prov.: _____
Telephone: _____ Country: _____ Zip: _____

**Visit us on the web at www.Foxchapelpublishing.com
or call us at 800-457-9112**

AFB00

From:_____
_____
City: _____
State/Prov.:_____
Country: _____Zip:_____

Scroll Saw
Work Shop
The How-To Magazine for Scrollers

1970 Broad St.
East Petersburg PA 17520   USA

From:_____
_____
City: _____
State/Prov.:_____
Country: _____Zip:_____

Wood Carving
I L L U S T R A T E D

1970 Broad St.
East Petersburg PA 17520   USA

From:_____
_____
City: _____
State/Prov.:_____
Country: _____Zip:_____

Fox
Chapel Publishing Co. Inc.

Free Catalog Offer
1970 Broad St.
East Petersburg PA 17520   USA